Lepidopterology

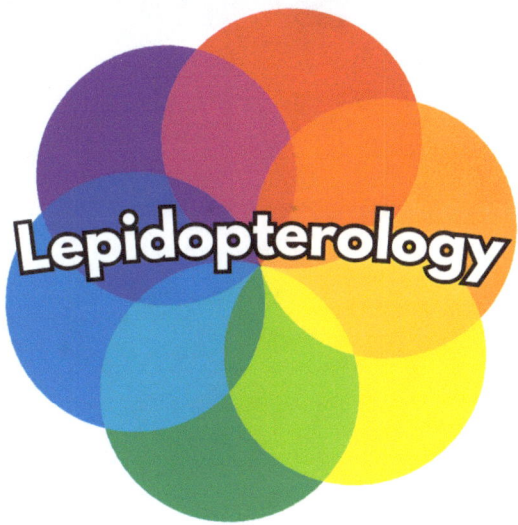

Book of COLORS

A Rainbow of Butterflies and Moths

Jessica Lee Anderson

Paperback ISBN: 978-1-964078-42-7

To Glen and Alfrieda, thanks for your kindness and support always! - JLA

Butterflies and moths are often multi-colored, so have fun pointing out all of the colors in addition to the featured colors!

Photo credits, left to right, top to bottom: Front cover: Billyboy13 (Peacock butterfly); Interior cover: Coopder1 (Atlas moth); Copyright page: leekris (Tobacco hornworm); Dedication page: Macropixel, Cathy Keifer; p. 4: Stephane Bidouze; Adam Pearson, Mirko_Rosenau; p. 5: igabriela, Erica Joy Photgraphy, Imnature; p. 6: GaborBalla, Rbemish, TonyBaggett; p. 7: Carolina Birdman, Heather Cutchin, aaprophoto; p. 8: photosbyjimn, Timothy Loyd, Rosemarie_Kappler; p. 9: johnandersonphoto, leekris, Ribeirodos Santos; p. 10: fntproject, ZoomTravels, nickkurzenko; p. 11: Brett_Hondow, Adrian Coleman, fotoedu; p. 12: Scott Walmsley Photography, ephotocorp, dopeyden; p. 13: Robert Kery, thomaszsebok, MC Yeung; p. 14: flicimage, milehightraveler, Andyworks; p. 15: Geobacillus, Daniel E Rieck's Images, Adisak Mitrprayoon; p. 16: Neil Bowman, Wirestock, Susie3Ford; p. 17: macrophotos, KalypsoWorldPhotography, Ian_Redding; p. 18: bookguy, Vinicius de Souza, Thomas Elliott; p. 19: Ian_Redding, David Hansche, Vinicius de Souza; p. 20: sstaton, Rod Hill, Brad Cox; p. 21: Paul_Cooper, GK005, Mantonature; p. 22: TrichopCMU, Mantonature, Peter Holmboe; p. 23: Ian_Redding, randimal, bookguy; p. 24: Sarah2, photonewman, Hans; p. 25: marcouliana, Ian_Redding, David Byron Keener; p. 26: happykamill, Ramapriya Rajagopalan, Cathy Keifer; p. 27: Paula French, teptong, Vah; p. 28: Jason Ondreicka, u_fpxb14xkjl, Jason Ondreicka; p. 29: teptong, macropixel, Thomas Elliott; p.30: Nicole Gilbo, stanley45; p. 31: Science Photo Library, Mathisa_s, LoggaWiggler; p. 32: missisya, hugocorzo, benjarattanapakee; p. 33: marcophotos, Shaun Wilkinson, sinseeho; p. 34: Michael Anderson; Back cover: Boonchuay_Promjiam (Blue pansy butterfly)

This Book Belongs to:

_____

Lepidopterology is the study of moths and butterflies.

Clipper butterfly

Cecropia moth

Red

Red lacewing butterfly

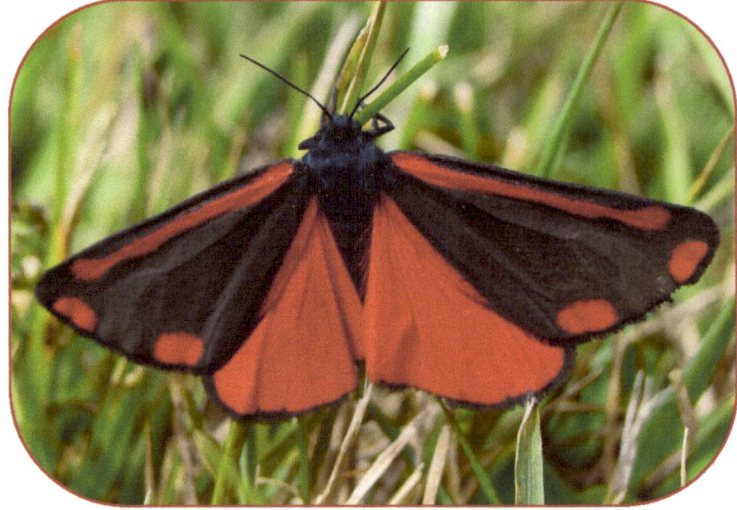

Cinnabar moth

Butterflies and moths are both types of insects that belong to the same order, Lepidoptera.

Scarlet peacock butterfly

Red

Scarlet tiger moth

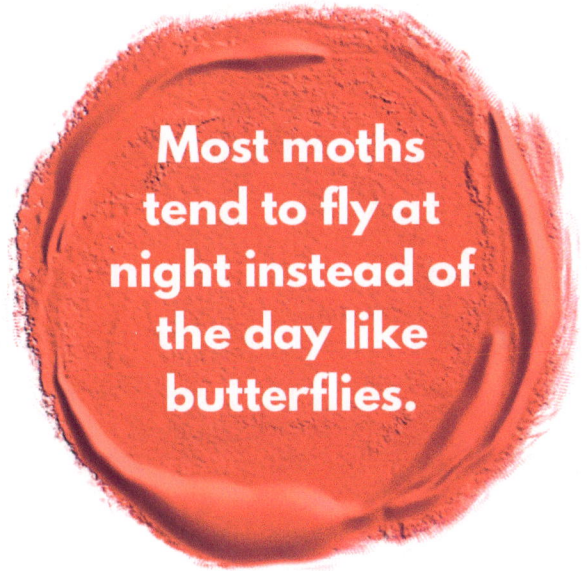

Most moths tend to fly at night instead of the day like butterflies.

Postman butterfly

Red admiral butterfly

Orange

Orange moth

Question mark butterfly

Moths and butterflies have antennae—long appendages at the top of their heads.

Gatekeeper butterfly

Orange

Gulf fritillary butterfly

Antennae help butterflies and moths smell and to also stay balanced.

Monarch butterfly

Painted lady butterfly

Yellow

Swallowtail butterfly

Southern dogface butterfly

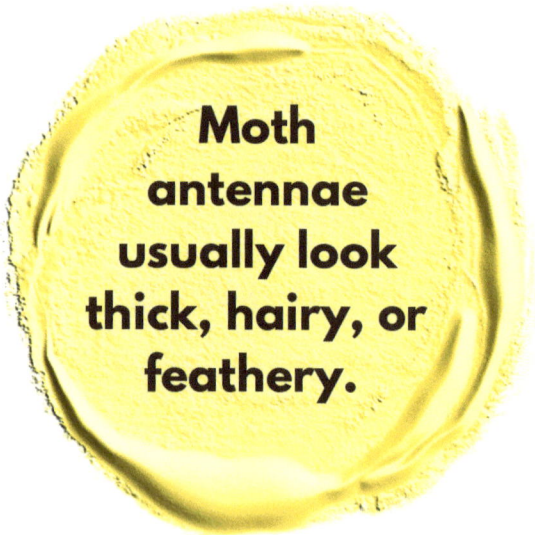

Moth antennae usually look thick, hairy, or feathery.

Brimstone moth

Yellow

Clouded sulphur butterfly

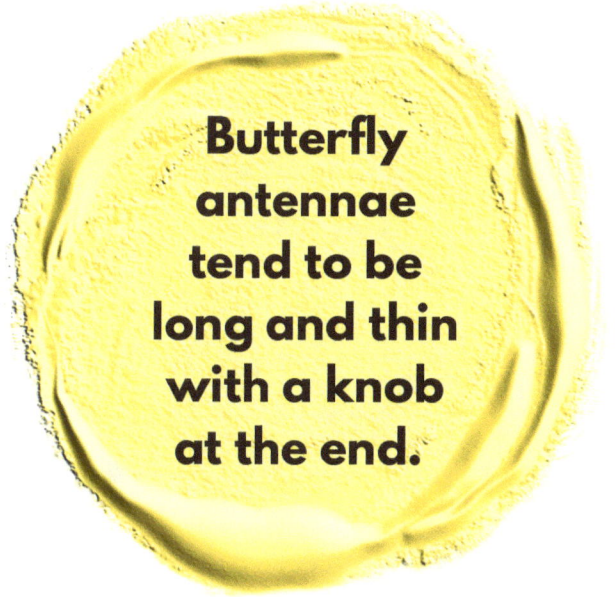

Butterfly antennae tend to be long and thin with a knob at the end.

Little yellow butterfly

Common grass yellow butterfly

Green

Dido longwing butterfly

Emerald swallowtail butterfly

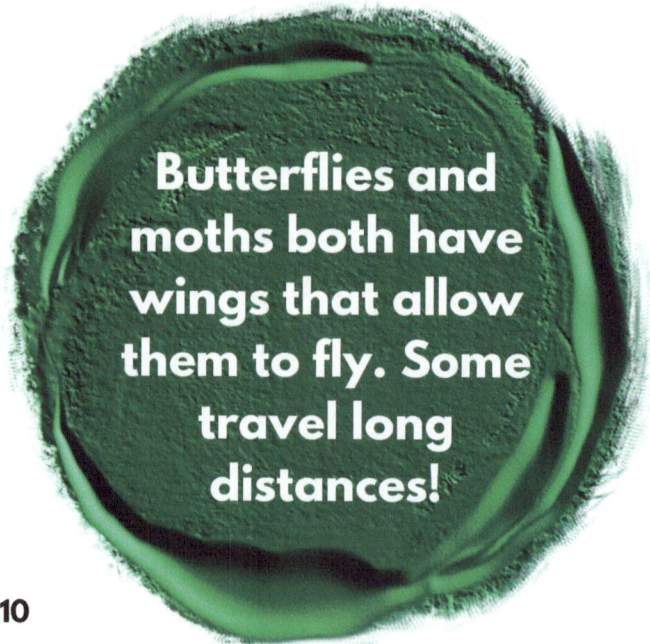

Butterflies and moths both have wings that allow them to fly. Some travel long distances!

Luna moth

Green

Large emerald moth

Butterfly wings rest upright and closed, unlike moths that have wings that rest spread open.

Green hairstreak butterfly

Malachite butterfly

Blue

Butterflies and moths can be a variety of colors and have different types of patterns.

Blue morpho

Blue tiger moth

Lowi swallowtail

Blue

Ulysses butterfly

Common blue butterfly

Gram blue butterfly

Their colors are created by tiny scales that reflect light. (Lepidoptera means "scale-winged").

Purple

Mint moth

Colorado hairstreak butterfly

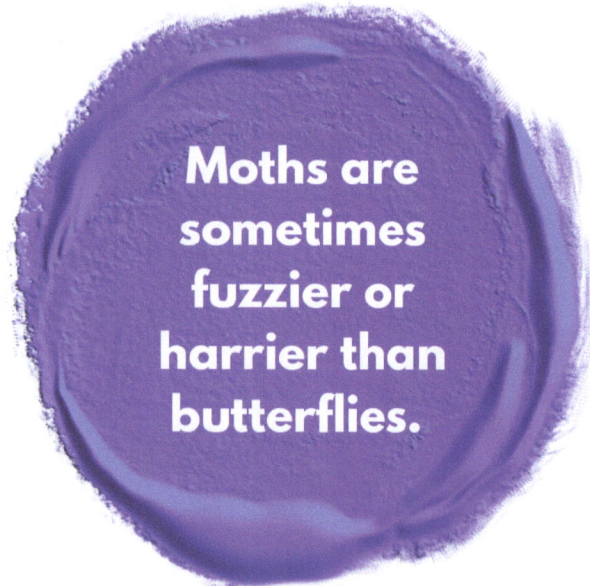

Moths are sometimes fuzzier or harrier than butterflies.

Lesser purple emperor butterfly

Purple

Great purple emperor butterfly

Some butterflies have slender bodies while moths tend to be thicker.

Southern purple mint moth

Purple leaf blue butterfly

Pink

Elephant hawk moth

Ruby-spotted swallowtail

Like other insects, moths and butterflies have four wings and six legs.

Six-spot burnet moth

Pink

Raspberry pyrausta moth

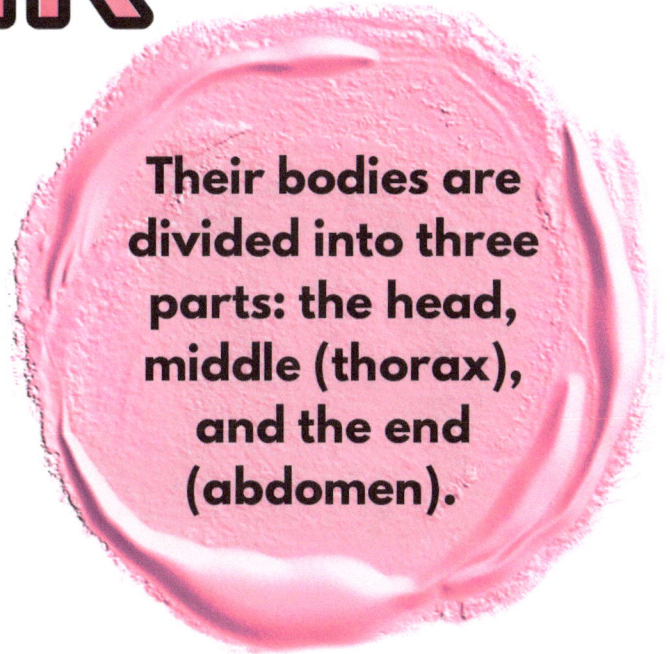

Their bodies are divided into three parts: the head, middle (thorax), and the end (abdomen).

Cattleheart butterfly

Rosy footman moth

Black

Mourning cloak butterfly

Black witch moth

There are more moths that exist than butterflies (about 160,000 moth species and 17,500 butterfly species).

Black swallowtail

Black

Peppered moth

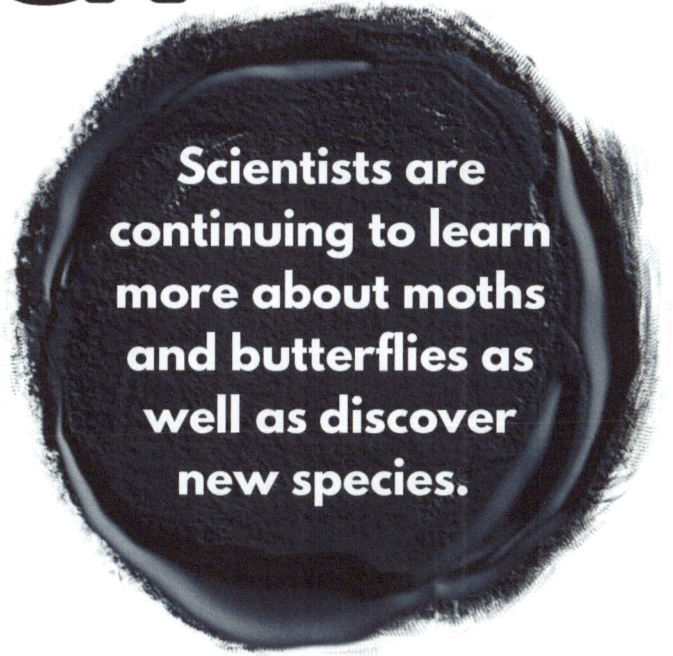

Scientists are continuing to learn more about moths and butterflies as well as discover new species.

Spangle butterfly

Sphinx moth

White

Checkered white butterfly

White satin moth

Most butterflies and moths drink nectar from flowers, but some eat other things like tree sap, rotting fruit, and even poop.

Cabbage white butterfly

White

Small white butterfly

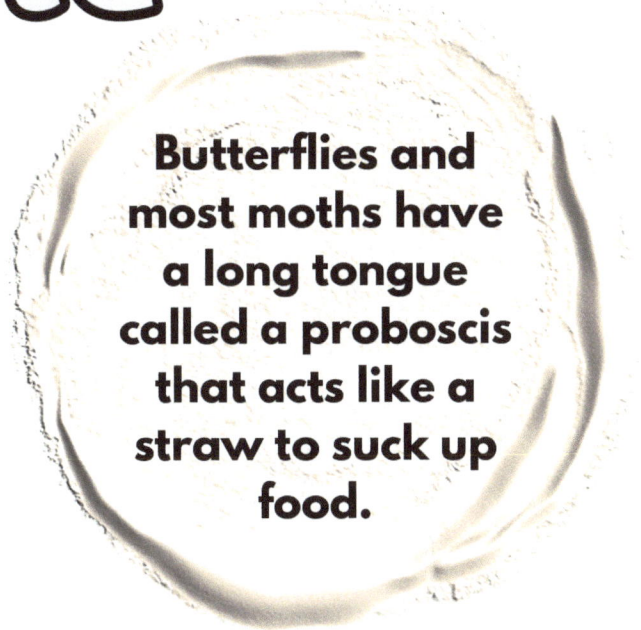

Butterflies and most moths have a long tongue called a proboscis that acts like a straw to suck up food.

Great southern white butterfly

White ermine moth

Gray

American snout butterfly

Peppered moth

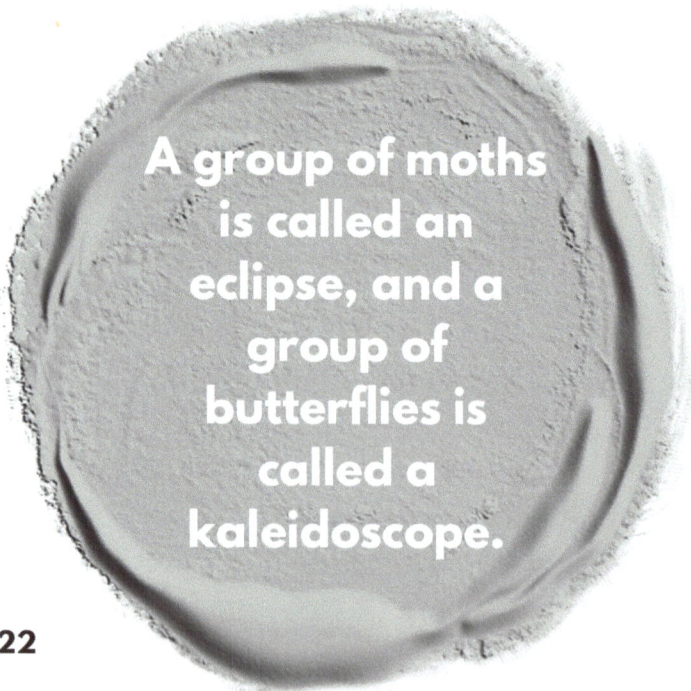

A group of moths is called an eclipse, and a group of butterflies is called a kaleidoscope.

Ringlet butterfly

Gray

Gray dagger moth

Butterflies and moths are important pollinators—they transfer pollen between plants, helping produce fruits and seeds.

Gray hairstreak butterfly

Little wood satyr butterfly

Brown

Speckled wood butterfly

Orange oak leaf butterfly

Butterflies and moths are important to the environment and food chain.

Brown atlas moth

Brown

Silk moth

Butterflies and moths are often symbols of hope and beauty because of their colors, patterns, and unique life cycle.

Pebble hook-tip moth

Eyed brown butterfly

COLOR Combinations

Butterflies and moths lay eggs to reproduce. Can you describe these colors and patterns?

Paper kite butterfly laying eggs

Painted jezebel laying eggs

Cecropia moth laying eggs

COLOR Combinations

Cabbage white butterfly eggs

Leopard lacewing butterfly eggs

Common green birdwing butterfly eggs

What are some things you notice about the shapes, colors, and features of these butterfly eggs?

COLOR Combinations

The caterpillar (larva) is the second stage of a butterfly or moth's life cycle.

Cecropia moth caterpillar

Saddleback moth caterpillar

Spicebush swallowtail butterfly caterpillar

COLOR Combinations

Drury's jewel moth caterpillar

Black swallowtail butterfly caterpillar

Monarch butterfly caterpillar

What are some things you notice about the shapes, colors, and features of these caterpillars?

COLOR Combinations

Caterpillars become pupa before transitioning to become adult butterflies or moths.

Monarch butterfly chrysalis (pupa) close-up

Transition from caterpillar to pupa to adult butterfly (metamorphosis)

COLOR Combinations

Painted lady butterfly chrysalis

Atlas moth cocoon

Silk moth cocoon

What are some things you notice about the shapes, colors, and features of the chrysalis and cocoons?

COLOR Combinations

Can you describe the colors and patterns of these butterflies?

Leopard lacewing butterfly

Anna's eighty-eight butterfly

Clipper butterfly

COLOR Combinations

Polyphemus moth

Great orange tip butterfly

Rajah Brooke's birdwing butterfly

Why do you think butterfly and moth colors, patterns, and shapes matter?

33

Jessica Lee Anderson is an award-winning author of over 75 books for young readers including the NAOMI NASH chapter book series. Jessica loves spending time in nature and exploring the outdoors with her husband, Michael, and their daughter, Ava! Jessica loves admiring butterflies and moths (especially monarchs) near her home in Austin, Texas. You can learn more about Jessica by visiting www.jessicaleeanderson.com.

Check out these other books:

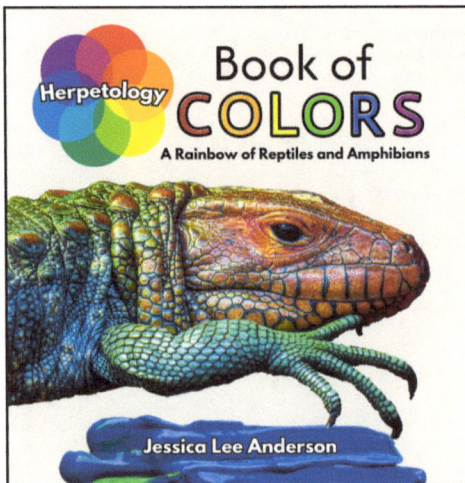

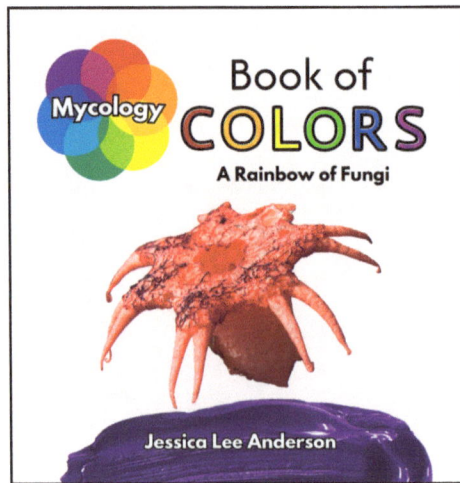

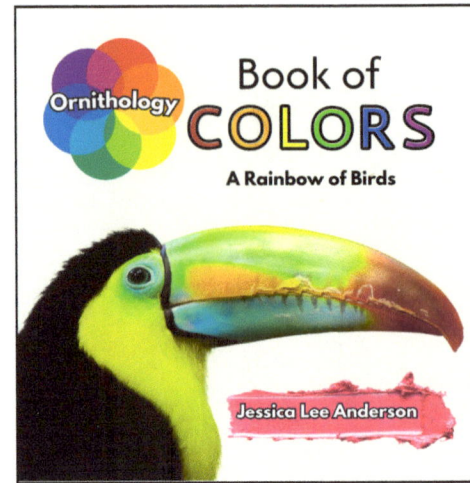

Herpetology
Book of COLORS
A Rainbow of Reptiles and Amphibians
Jessica Lee Anderson

Mycology
Book of COLORS
A Rainbow of Fungi
Jessica Lee Anderson

Ornithology
Book of COLORS
A Rainbow of Birds
Jessica Lee Anderson

www.ingramcontent.com/pod-product-compliance
Lightning Source LLC
Chambersburg PA
CBHW061145030426
42335CB00002B/103

* 9 7 8 1 9 6 4 0 7 8 4 2 7 *